Beautiful Ruins

Verses of Love, Longing and Life....

Kriti Tuteja

Copyright © Kriti Tuteja
All Rights Reserved.

This book has been self-published with all reasonable efforts taken to make the material error-free by the author. No part of this book shall be used, reproduced in any manner whatsoever without written permission from the author, except in the case of brief quotations embodied in critical articles and reviews.

The Author of this book is solely responsible and liable for its content including but not limited to the views, representations, descriptions, statements, information, opinions, and references ["Content"]. The Content of this book shall not constitute or be construed or deemed to reflect the opinion or expression of the Publisher or Editor. Neither the Publisher nor Editor endorse or approve the Content of this book or guarantee the reliability, accuracy, or completeness of the Content published herein and do not make any representations or warranties of any kind, express or implied, including but not limited to the implied warranties of merchantability, fitness for a particular purpose.

The Publisher and Editor shall not be liable whatsoever...

Made with ❤ on the BookLeaf Publishing Platform
www.bookleafpub.in
www.bookleafpub.com

Dedication

For every heart that has loved, lost, and still dares to hope.
For love - in its beginnings, endings, and in-betweens.
And for those I loved, lost, and learnt from - you live within these lines...

Preface

This collection is a journey through the many shades of the human heart. Each poem is born from moments of love and longing, of heartbreak and healing, of inspiration and quiet reflection. Together, they weave fragments of lived experience into verses that speak of what it means to feel deeply and live fully.

These poems are not bound by time or place; they are simply the echoes of emotions that every soul encounters at some point. I hope that as you turn these pages, you find pieces of your own story mirrored in these lines, and perhaps a sense of comfort, connection, or courage.

This book is an offering - from one heart to another.

Acknowledgements

This book would not have been possible without the unwavering love and strength of both my mothers - *Madhu Tuteja* and *Soniya Checker* - whose faith has been my anchor through every high and low. My muse, *Manjhi*, who walked beside me through life's shadows and light, revealing emotions I never knew I held, helping me understand life, and inspiring the words that now dwell within these pages. My life's experiences - the joys, heartbreaks, and lessons etched along the way - have shaped the depth and heartbeat of this collection.

The title, *Beautiful Ruins*, found its spark in the hauntingly tender song written by Freddy Wexler and performed by Ashley Park, whose melody and words mirrored my own reflections on love, loss, and hope.

Finally, to everyone who has walked with me, whether in fleeting moments or enduring bonds - thank you for leaving traces that live within these pages.

1. The Power within You

The beauty in you,
The power that you possess,
Is what you think;
Is what that helps you progress.

As you sow,
So shall you reap,
Is that one phrase;
That will help you achieve.

No dream is too big,
No goal is too high,
That can make you ponder;
Or that can make you sigh.

Have faith in yourself,
Then create a vision,
Center your energies;
And kick start that mission.

Everything around you,
Was once just a thought,
And with this one realization;
All the mysteries will be sought.

Go back in time,
Recall that moment,
When your earnest wish;
Was fulfilled by a comet.

That comet made you ask,
That comet made you believe,
That comet developed your faith;
But what made you achieve?

It is You all over,
It is You every time,
It was You that attracted it;
It was You, and your Mind.

So rise up, oh dreamer,
Let your spirit take flight,
For the beauty in you;
Is a beacon of light.

2. I Heard a Voice

Deep in thoughts,
I was pondering alone;
To struggle hard,
Or to go back home.

I heard a voice,
sweet and crisp;
Filled with life,
Love and lift.

Like a gentle breeze,
After a scorching sun;
Like a drop of rain,
After a drought has come.

It filled me with ecstasy,
I lost my thoughts;
It blessed me with light,
And my problems were sought.

I ran after it,
But I lost my way;
Only to realize,
That I was on my grave.

Yet whispers linger,
In shadows they play;
The echoes of hope,
Refusing to fray.

With every heartbeat,
A spark would ignite;
Guiding me gently,
Through the depth of the night.

For every lost moment,
A chance to reclaim;
To rise from my ashes,
And dance in the flame.

3. I am a Lady, for I had a Queen

Living in a place,
Where women are looked down upon.
You gave me a space,
Where that woman in me saw its dawn.

The wish to be;
Among but, out of the crowd;
Developed within me,
And today you can be proud.

Am blessed to have you,
A lady first then a Queen.
As you knew how to brew;
Values for a fine gleam.

I have knowledge,
For you had wisdom.
I have courage,
For you had a vision.

I owe to you my Queen,
For my heart is your territory;
Which you nurtured with care,

The fruits of which, I always share.

I bow to you my Queen,
For my mind is your subject;
Which you never did dictate,
And the wings of which, made me rare.

I am a Lady;
For I had a Queen,
A woman in her true essence;
Mother, you are my dream.

4. Kites....

Hustle and bustle everywhere,
No sign of content and rest.
Sounds of horns jamming my ears,
The sweet melody of birds lost somewhere.

Bright lights instead of the moon;
Conditioned air instead of a cool breeze;
Sounds of construction instead of rustling leaves;
Heavens! Where I have been...

Doubtful eyes haunting me,
Of who can I be?
Some seem busy with themselves,
And some busy trespassing.

Restricting me to myself,
Why I can't just dance carefree.
Killing my desires for someone,
Someone who will never be.

My life seems like a kite,
Controlled by the demands of the society;
Wishing, waiting, longing for a storm,
To cut and set me free.

And as the night falls;
Gleaming lights laugh at my thoughts.
As a storm can only destroy;
Displacing you to lands unknown,

Alas! There I need to be...

5. A World in Total Darkness

If only I could see, see the world in total darkness,
It may seem colorless; but will have the color of total freedom.
Freedom to be what you really want to be,
Without the fear of observing eyes; haunting every move of yours,
While ignoring the charisma in abound.

If only I could see, see the world in total darkness,
The sound of birds and the touch of leaves,
The feel of the gentle breeze;
Will never fade away unheard; unfelt,
But will be the base - the canvas of my life, my mind.

If only I could see, see the world in total darkness,
The light within me will have a chance to flourish,
Expanding my reach; widening my thoughts;
Giving me a better picture,
A picture; eyes wide open cannot see.

A world in total darkness, can always be an ideal one,
For it gives us a scope to brighten up our lives, our mind.
As a canvas waits in patience to be stroked with pangs of

imagination;
The world inside you dark with ignorance awaits its dawn,
The dawn of its glorification, Elevation!

6. Quest for Lost Self

Who am I,
What am I to become?
That spark they say,
Has gone down in sum.

Change is inevitable,
As inevitable as death;
But how can a change,
Make the person lose his strength?

I had a life,
A goal to achieve;
But the quenched desire realized,
It was so baseless and weak.

Who am I,
What am I to become?
The thing that I ran for,
Impoverished my rhythm.

Who am I to seek,
To guide me what to do?
Is it my soul within,
Or a wise guru?

My inner space is crowded,
With many expectations and thoughts.
The voice has succumbed politely;
Owing to the preferences around.

I beseech you my Lord,
Revive me, take my hand;
I don't want to become,
What I already have.

Show me the path,
Where my spirit can soar;
Lift the veil of silence,
Let my true self restore.

For in the depths of sorrow,
A flicker still ignites;
A yearning for the light,
To guide me through the nights.

Who am I,
In this mirror of fate?
A wanderer seeking,
To rewrite what's innate...

7. A Soul's Cry

Let me be free,
Because I have my own wishes...
Just don't restrict me,
To the un-cleaned dishes...

Let me sore high,
Let me touch the sky,
Let me live my life;
And please don't ask me why?

Even if you will ask;
Why I can't do such a task?
I'll just simply smile and say;
My creator let me have my way...

Let me have my way,

Let me chase the dawn,
Where my visions ignite,
For a heart that is free,
Is a heart full of light.

8. Intoxication

The world seems to be on cloud nine,
You don't care what you hear or whine;
Intoxication gives you a feeling,
That all your wounds are healing.

You live in a place that's for you to rule;
And no-one seems to be so rude!
With ear plugs in your ears,
You hear only what you want to hear.

The crowd around then ceases to exist;
When you have the bliss that intoxication gives.
You don't care who you touch; you are not as conscious as before;
While in intoxication the freedom is there to feel so awkwardly secure...

You become so bold;
That no one dares to behold,
The powerful becomes merely weak;
As an introvert becomes the voice of his being...

Your eyes speak more; as they only connect to the world around,

But the mind has gone; to a world where only you belong.
Stress is nowhere close; calm is all you feel,
That's the power of intoxication; that only to the blessed is revealed.

You bloody don't care what you look or other's say,
When intoxication has engulfed you in its embrace.
Hey don't worry; there is no harm to feel this way,
When all your life you do exactly how others want you to behave.

You don't bloody care who is around you,
As you are lost in the energy that surrounds you.
You feel as if you are an audience to a play called life,
Where the actors play their parts, and you just sit - free from strife...

9. Our Fragile Heart

I met a girl
Wild and free
She was rebellious
But her heart was weak.

She took life as it came
Enjoying every bit of it
Only to realize in the end
That there was nothing authentic about it.

Heartbroken she roamed around
Trying to find what was her crime
A fake smile adorned her face
While her heart traveled back in time.

While finding reasons
Of where she went wrong
She met someone
Who pushed her beyond.

He rekindled the spark
Brightened her days
And cared for her
In his own silly ways.

While she ascended towards
Her newly found life
I smiled and thought,
"Why a girl's heart is so fragile?"

We love a total stranger
With all our might
Easily falling to every trap
Without thinking of what is right.

When heart broken
We take another risk
The adventure in our life
How can we even miss.

All that we want
Is love, time and care
This is what fools us best
And this is what makes our love rare.

10. I was Waiting to be Found

I was waiting to be found,
In a world that goes around,
Like nothing is there beyond,
I was waiting to be found by you....

I was waiting for a life,
With no sorrow or strife,
Only love around in rife,
I was waiting for a life with you....

I was waiting to be loved,
Like I am your flesh and blood,
Till I go down in mud,
I was waiting to be loved by you....

And now I long no more,
For I have found my shore,
You are the one I adore,
I am glad that I was found by you....

11. The Way I Love You

How much I love you;
Words cannot express,
The feelings of heart;
Only the eyes can reflect.

Eyes are a doorway;
A doorway to the soul,
Where true feelings reside;
Waiting to be explored.

There is a sigh of relief;
Whenever I feel you near me,
And my body brims with pleasure;
Whenever you touch me.

Without the sound of your funny laugh;
The day seems incomplete,
And just that smile on your face;
Made me taste my glorious defeat.

A simple stroll across the road;
Hand in hand makes me sway,
And I wish these moments never ends;
That is what I always pray.

Your irritating talks make me furious;
Though it always acts as a guide,
And this is what always made me curious;
That how it ever comes to your silly mind.

A simple gesture;
A sweet smile,
Many tokens of love;
And, fights all the time.

This is what makes us going;
This is what retains our trust,
This is what brings us near;
This is what proves us just.

How much I love you;
How can I even express?
Because words are not enough;
To convey the longing in every breath.

12. How Can I Leave Him?

How can I leave him;
When he was there and you were not?

When the path was tough,
He was the only one to trust.

When the thorns were spread,
He was the only one who led.

When the storm broke,
He was the only one for support.

When the trial was on,
He was the only one to rely on.

When the sadness overcame,
He was the only one who made me gay.

When there was no solution,
He was the only one who build my resolution.

When my identity failed,
He was the only one who made it regained.

When the dreams were black,
He was the only one who drew their colors back.

How can I leave him?

As he taught me how to mend my sorrows,
And guided me out of the deadly hollows.

With him my joy doubles;
And there are no signs of troubles.

He is the only one who knows my deep dark secrets,
And I am the one who has his leaflet.

By knowing him I feel as if I know myself,
As he's the only one who urges me to go beyond self.

With him my imaginations have no bounds,
And I can be a human amongst the hounds.

His self-less love made me pure,
Who now everyone adores.

He accepts me as I am,
And demands nothing but a thought.

So tell me, how can I leave him;
When he was there; and you were not?

13. My Life Itself Had No Meaning

My life went on; on a chose path,
But perplexed and diffused;
My mind needed another start...

While strolling towards the destined way,
My mind encountered its destiny,
Its bay...

You my lord were sitting there,
A stranger to me,
But my heart did sway...

A stir in the soul and my mind got the clue,
That you were the one,
Destiny had kept for due...

Four in the morning, but the conversation went on,
And the pain from the thud on my head,
Already gone...

We were so distant; yet so close,
You became the muse,
Of my prose...

I was your mirror and you were mine,
Yet so hollow,
Alas! Divine...

You took me to a whole new world,
Relished my soul;
Registered your every word...

But,

As time went by; the priorities changed,
To stand up to the world,
My soul did pay...

I worked hard by your motto; tried to add meaning to my life,
But my soul always cried,
As it had no meaning without you in my life...

You are my dream; a dream that can never come true,
As fantasy is an escape,
An escape from the bitter truth...

Alas my lord!
Be my dream; so that I can escape into you,
But be not a reality; I may escape you...

14. A Solidarity Brief

It was a moment;
A solidarity brief,
When I had you;
And you had me.

I was in a flux;
As my destiny was defined,
But seeing you there;
I wanted to defy.

I took one step;
And you took three,
And for a moment there I thought;
That you could set me free...

You asked me to stay;
To which I did obey,
Lonely as we both were;
That moment made us sway.

Soon your fingers;
Developed a taste,
Thrilled my body;
Resisted to the haste.

It is not even a year now;
But still I remember those days;
When I was your betrothed;
And then bequeath was conveyed...

Memories of the past;
Slaps hard on my face,
When now after death;
Am bound to live again.

It was a moment;
A solidarity brief,
But I still get a glimpse;
Of the unseen grief.

15. Hello

There is something that I wanted to say,
My heart is sinking to have you away,
Just wanted to hear your voice and live again,
…..The number you are calling is not responding…..

It's been more than an hour last I struck your bell,
Wondering if you really saw that missed call in your cell,
Hope this time my ailing heart will be lucky,
….The number you are calling is busy….

Minutes to hours and hours to day,
I never heard from you back hope you are ok,
My body shivers from that eerie thought,
….The number you are calling is switched off….

How hopeless our relationship has become,
Do you really remember that I used to be the one?
Just for once pick up the phone;
Before my final call takes me home…

Hello….. Puna…..

…………………………………………………………………………………..

16. Past Calling

The moment I thought;
That I had moved on,
My past came knocking;
And there you were.

You brought along with you;
The silly days of past,
Which made me laugh;
As long did they last.

Just a glimpse of you;
And I travelled back in time,
Living each day in every second;
And each tear in every smile.

It took me years;
Years no less than a century,
To go beyond the phase;
Which seemed as an eternity.

But now as I stand;
Back from where I begun,
My mind started to question;
"Does it really need to be done?"

Some meek hopes build;
As you walked by my side,
And the moment I left your aura;
Reality struck back hard but; Light!

Blinded for a moment;
Now the vision is wide and clear,
That you my friend;
Was never mine; never near.

You taught me many a things,
Things I never thought I had in me:

The patience to wait,
The power to hold back,
The strength to set you free, and
The ability to love selflessly.

The past with you was a lesson;
Good or bad, time has yet to decide.
As many a things are still left unlearned;
Maybe that's why you came back in my life...

17. Since When?

The time moved on fast;
I couldn't keep a track,
Since when we became Us;
And from us, You and I back again?

We always had something to share;
To teach, to show, to explore.
And now all that we can say;
Is what You and I had ignored.

The tables so suddenly turned around;
I didn't feel the pace,
Since when the melody of your voice;
Became the noise of your stakes?

Our eyes used to speak more;
I still remember the day,
When sitting in a garden of wonder;
Our lost eyes never did sway.

My trust, respect and love;
Fell down on the ground face first,
Since when the innocence of your talks;
Became so centered beneath the crust?

I don't want to recall the past;
It hurts to feel like a fool,
Putting everything on the edge I came;
Now back home, with nothing left to lose...

18. Role Reversals

From sunny days to the darkest nights,
From disarray to the world of might,
I have been through all; I have seen it through,
Your hell for me was a boon to prove.

Heat weakens the metal;
While water gives it strength,
The struggle in between;
Is what shapes it best.

The blows of your deeds;
The aim of your words,
Struck through my heart;
And wounded my soul.

In the comfort of time;
The truth was revealed,
A journey through hell;
Gave me ecstasy indeed!

Am complete in myself;
You proved my metal,
Now it's time to go beyond;
And brew my kettle.

So here I stand;
Unshackled and free,
With forged resolve;
And a heart full of glee.

The furnace of pain;
Has turned into light,
As I gather my dreams:
Taking flight into night.

Each spark of my spirit;
Like stars in the dawn,
Illuminates pathways;
Where shadows were drawn.

I'll gather the moments;
That once held me small,
And weave them together;
A tapestry tall.

19. Salvation!

Everything is destined
Each moment is planned
Intuitions and sign that you get
The calling of your heart
All stitched together
Feet pulling you to a path unknown
A path leading to your destiny
A moment in a life, a life in a moment
When your being is void
When your identity is lost
Realization of the true self
Every other thing is materialized
What are you here for?
To earn, learn, marry
Or to go for that one journey
That will end the remaining to come

Salvation!!!

20. पुकारती ज़िन्दगी

अपनी ही मस्ती में मगरूर थे हम,
ना साथी, ना रहगुज़र की तलाश थी।
समझते थे हम जिसको ज़िन्दगी;
वो काँच के महल की तरह थी।

दूर कहीं आहट हुई;
फिर एक दस्तक,
थम सी गई साँसें मेरी;
और टूट गई दीवारें।

ज़मीन पर बिखरे थे कुछ भ्रम मेरे,
पर हर दिशा में फैली दिखी;
चमकती रौशनी पुकारती हुई।

डर है कहीं चोट न लगे,
संभल के बढ़ा रही हूँ पाँव।
दूर रौशनी चकाचौंध है,
पर राह नहीं आसान।

21. बदलती तस्वीर
(खुद से खुदकी पहचान)

तुमसे मिली तो खुदको जाना,
जिन रंगों से सजी हूँ, उनको पहचाना।
हर एक तिनके की पहचान कराई,
उनसे जुड़ी एक तस्वीर बनाई।

तस्वीर थी वो जैसे एक पहेली,
सदियों से तन्हा थी वो अकेली।
समय की मार पड़ी तो धूल की आगोश में,
समेटती गई खुदको वो किसी की आस में।

कितने ही आए निहारने उसे,
कितने ही आए निखारने उसे,
कितने ही आए पाने उसे,
पर कोई न आया अपनाने उसे।

दूसरों की चाह में रंगते-रंगते,
अपने ही असल रंग भूल गई थी वो।
दूसरों के अरमानों में ढलते-ढलते,
अपना ही वजूद खो बैठी थी वो।

देखो! आज कई दिनों बाद,
हुई है फिर एक दस्तक।

धुंधलाया सा दिख रहा है एक चेहरा,
घने बालों से सजा, कुछ जुदा।

कुछ लम्हे ही तो बीते थे,
ज़रा सी धूल ही तो छंटी थी,
फिर आया एक फरमान, नीलामी का,
पर फिर भी खुश हूँ मैं।

खुश हूँ कि अपना पाई हूँ खुदको,
भले कोई अपनाये, या न अपनाये।
खुश हूँ कि जी सकी हूँ तेरी आँखों में,
अब मौत आए, या बे-मौत ही मर जाएँ।

22. मैं क्यों थम गया

इस ज़िन्दगी की रफ़्तार में,
चहल-पहल और भागदौड़ में,
बुझ रही थी लौ मेरी,
बिन किसी मुकाम के।

एक जूनून था जो सर मेरे,
एक जोश था जो मन मेरे,
ढला जा रहा था वो कहीं,
बदली हुई सी सोच में।

मैं इस लिये खड़ा रहा;
के तुम मुझे पुकार लो,
पुकार कर दुलार लो;
दुलार कर सवाँर लो।

ये वक़्त इसलिये है थम गया;
के तुम इसे विचार लो,
विचार कर सुधार लो;
सुधार कर निखार लो।

23. तुम्हारी क्रिती

तेरी नज़रों की मैं एहसानमंद हूँ,
मैं खुशनसीब हूँ कि मैं तुझे पसंद हूँ।

तेरे लफ़्ज़ बयां न कर सकें जो,
मैं उन ख़यालों की कहानी सी हूँ।

तेरे लबों से मिलकर रौशनी में तबदील हो जाए जो,
मैं उस मचलते हुए प्यासे परवाने सी हूँ।

तेरे एहसास से मिलकर निखर जाए जो,
ऐ भंवरे, मैं उस गुलिस्तां सी हूँ।

अपने चाँद को अपनी गोद में रखे हुए है जो,
मैं उस ठहरे हुए पानी सी हूँ।

शबनमी बूँदों को समेटती जाए जो,
मैं उस तपती हुई ज़मीन सी हूँ।

सूने आँगन में गूँज जाए जो,
मैं उस बेलगाम हँसी सी हूँ।

तेरे आगोश में घर बनाए है जो,
मैं उस नन्ही परी सी हूँ।

तेरी राह को सदा तकती है जो,
मैं उन बोझल निगाहों सी हूँ।

तेरी चाह से हर रोज़ पनपते हैं जो,
मैं उन बेहिसाब ख़्वाहिशों सी हूँ।

आ, पूरा कर दे मुझे, पूर्णिमा हो जाऊँ,
ये एहसान कर दे कि फना हो जाऊँ।

24. गुफ्तगू

तेरी और मेरी बातों की मैं किताब लिख दूँ,
हमारी गुफ्तगू में सुलझते हुए नग्मे-ए-हयात लिख दूँ।

ना दिन का पता हो, ना वक्त का होश,
इस कायनात के खुलते हुए रहस्यों में यूँ मदहोश।

तेरी सोहबत में जो मिलता है मुझे ज़िन्दगी का सबब,
हर रोज याद दिलाता है मुझे जीने का अदब।

25. राहत

आज हवाओं में कुछ ठंडी राहत सी है,
और मेरे दिल में तेरी इक आहट सी है...

फ़िज़ा में बह रहा है गीली मिट्टी का एहसास,
और मुझे समेटे हुए है तेरा ही लिबास...

बारिश की सर्गम में झूम उठा है समा,
और मेरे ख़याल तुझमें हो रहे हैं फना...

कभी थमते, कभी चलते, कभी बुझते, कभी जलते,
मेरे कदमों और तेरी यादों का बनता हुआ ताना-बाना।

ठहर गया है कहीं तुझसे होकर ये दूर,
पता ही ना चला कब हुए इतने मजबूर...

26. लास्ट सीन

तुझे देखे बरस बीत गए, तुझे सुने एक उम्र।
तेरे दीदार को तेरी तस्वीर भी ना मिली,
मिला तो बस *WhatsApp* का *last seen*...

तुम आज भी देर से सो कर; जल्दी उठ जाते हो।
दिन में हर घंटे चंद लम्हों के लिए ही सही,
ऑनलाइन आ जाते हो।

ऐसा बहुत बार हुआ है कि,
तुम्हारी प्रोफाइल देखने से क्षण भर पहले ही,
तुम आके जा चुके होते हो...

क्या जैसे मैं तुमको याद करती हूँ,
तुम भी मुझे याद करते हो???

उंगलियाँ टाइप करते-करते रुक जाती हैं,
पर तुमको टाइप करते भी तो नहीं देखा।

गर तेरा भी वही हाल है जो मेरा है,
तो फिर क्यों तू मुझसे बात नहीं करता....

एक अनचाहे, अनसोचे, अनमाँगे मोड़ से गुज़री है ज़िन्दगी,
दिल तेरा भी उतना ही दुखा है; जितना दर्द मुझमें समा है।

जानते हुए भी के अब पहले वाली बात ना रहेगी,
फिर भी ज़िन्दगी के इस खेल में;
एक दाँव और खेलने को दिल करता है...

27. दिल तड़प रहा है

दिल तड़प रहा है;
मचल रहा है;
आज फिर तेरी याद में,
ये बहक रहा है।

संजो रहा है;
वो यादें पुरानी,
कुछ कसमें, कुछ वादें;
कुछ ख्वाब रूमानी।

भूल गया था ये नादाँ;
जैसे कभी जिए ही न हों,
तेरे साथ के वो कश;
जैसे कभी पीये ही न हों।

फिर आज क्यों;
ये सैलाब उठा है,
मेरे जिस्म का हर कण;
तेरा ही नाम लेके गूँज उठा है।

नासमझ है ये;
झूठ को सच मान बैठा है।
यकीन हो चला है इसे;
के तू भी मेरा नाम ले बैठा है....

www.ingramcontent.com/pod-product-compliance
Lightning Source LLC
Chambersburg PA
CBHW070459050426
42449CB00012B/3048